AF751662

Photo: Sarah Hadley

SUZIE MILLER is a contemporary international playwright, librettist, screenwriter and novelist drawn to complex human stories often exploring injustice.

Miller has been produced around the world winning multiple prestigious awards. Most recently her play, *Prima Facie*, won three Australian Writers' Guild Awards and when it premiered in the West End, earned five-star reviews across all platforms, winning the London Olivier Awards 2023 for Best New Play, and Best Actor, winning the 2023 London Whatsonstage award for Best Play and winning the 2023 UK Southbank Sky Arts Award for best play and others. The same production opened on Broadway in 2023 earning four Tony nominations. *Prima Facie* has now been translated into over 20 languages, with productions all over the world and is being made into an international film.

Other award-winning and leading play credits include: *Jailbaby*; *Anna K*; *RBG: Of Many, One*; *Caress/Ache*; *Sunset Strip*; *Dust*; *SOLD*; *The Mathematics Of Longing*; *A Feminist Medea*; *Reasonable Doubt*; *Driving Into Walls* and *Cross Sections*.

Suzie has a background in law (she worked as a human rights and children's rights lawyer) and science, and is currently developing major theatre, film and television projects across the UK, US, and Australia.

Miller's first novel, *Prima Facie*, was published by Pan Macmillan in Australia in 2023 and will be published in the USA and UK in 2024.

RBG:

OF MANY, ONE

Suzie Miller

CURRENCY PRESS
The performing arts publisher

CURRENCY PLAYS

First published in 2024
by Currency Press
Gadigal Land, Suite 310, 46-56 Kippax Street, Surry Hills NSW 2010, Australia
enquiries@currency.com.au
www.currency.com.au

Copyright: *Ruth Bader Ginsburg: Writing law as a letter to the future* copyright © Karen O'Connell, 2024; *RBG: Of Many, One* copyright © Suzie Miller, 2024.

Copying for Educational Purposes

The Australian *Copyright Act 1968* [Act] allows a maximum of one chapter or 10% of this book, whichever is the greater, to be copied by any educational institution for its educational purposes provided that that educational institution [or the body that administers it] has given a remuneration notice to Copyright Agency [CA] under the Act.

For details of the CA licence for educational institutions contact CA, 12 / 66 Goulburn Street, Sydney, NSW, 2000; tel: within Australia 1800 066 844 toll free; outside Australia 61 2 9394 7600; fax: 61 2 9394 7601; email: memberservices@copyright.com.au

Copying for Other Purposes

Except as permitted under the Act, for example a fair dealing for the purposes of study, research, criticism or review, no part of this book may be reproduced, stored in a retrieval system, or transmitted in any form or by any means without prior written permission. All enquiries should be made to the publisher at the address above.

Any performance or public reading of *RBG: Of Many, One* is forbidden unless a licence has been received from the author or the author's agent. The purchase of this book in no way gives the purchaser the right to perform the play in public, whether by means of a staged production or a reading. All applications for public performance should be addressed to the author c / –HLA, email: hla@hlamgt.com.au, tel: 61 2 9549 3000.

Typeset by Brighton Gray for Currency Press.
Printed by CanPrint, Canberra, ACT.
Cover design by Katherine Zhang for Currency Press. Cover photo by Rene Vaile.

Currency Press acknowledges the Traditional Owners of the Country on which we live and work. We pay our respects to all Aboriginal and Torres Strait Islander Elders, past and present.

NATIONAL LIBRARY OF AUSTRALIA

A catalogue record for this book is available from the National Library of Australia

Contents

Heather Mitchell in Sydney Theatre Company's RBG: Of Many, One*, 2023 (Photo: Prudence Upton)*

Ruth Bader Ginsburg: Writing law as a letter to the future

'With law you can change things with words'

Can a single judge—one brilliant, determined woman—change the law to bring it closer to justice?

Suzie Miller's play, *RBG: Of Many, One*, tells the life, through vignettes from childhood to death, of the great American jurist Ruth Bader Ginsburg, known as 'RBG'. While it is a story of the triumphant legal career of a talented woman overcoming discrimination, the play also reveals, through the parameters of an individual life, deeper truths about law and justice.

'My dissenting judgments... are letters to the future'

The play begins with a metaphorical clock ticking. RBG is waiting for the phone call that will tell her whether she is to be appointed to the United States Supreme Court, the highest Court in America. She is willing time to pass in an agony of anticipation, while then-President Clinton delays making the call in order to watch a televised basketball game.

'Only a man could possibly think basketball is more important than the future of the Supreme Court.'

At the end of the play, elderly and sick with the cancer that will take her life, RBG wills time to slow: trying to keep death at bay with a disciplined exercise regime, holding on in hope of a change of government, and for her place on the bench to be filled by a Democratic party nominee who will continue her legacy.

Just as the play depicts an individual lifespan through a pastiche of remembered past and imagined future, law itself has an idiosyncratic relation to time. In the common law tradition, legal decisions made by judges become precedent, binding future legal actors. Over time these accretions become 'the law'. Each generation of judges lays down the next layer of case law, smoothing a messy multitude of possible decisions and choices into a single monolith. In this way, judicial acts of creation are obscured. This bestows upon law a veneer of inevitability that works against fundamental change.

And yet, *RBG* reveals a chink in the process of judging where the act of creation is exposed, and alternative futures are made possible. Dissenting judgments show that law is not, in fact, a monolith. The dissenting judgment, in which a judge presents an alternative take on the law and facts before them, may be the path not taken, but it demonstrates that another path was possible. In Miller's play, RBG comes fully into her power as a judge when she delivers a series of dissenting judgements, that do not sway the decision in the individual case, but influence legal thinking and political actions more broadly.

Over the past twenty years, in 'feminist judgments' projects around the world, scholars and equality advocates have similarly gathered to rewrite judicial decisions from a feminist perspective. Starting with the same constraints of precedent and legal limitation that apply to sitting judges, these reconceived judgments demonstrate that an alternative path through law is possible: one that foregrounds gender equality, as RBG's dissenting judgments did.

'One by one the women fall aside'

Why is this feminist rewriting of the law needed? Examples of gender injustice run through the play, along with RBG's outrage, carefully controlled so that anger does not undermine her success. RBG is repeatedly shut out of systems that were built for men. As a woman, she is not counted in the minyan for prayers at her mother's funeral, she is treated differently to male students at law school, and she lands her first legal job only after the intervention of a male professor. However highly qualified, for her, brilliance is not enough: her success still depends on the benevolence of the men in her life. RBG is married to Marty, a supportive and loving man, committed to sharing domestic work and childcare and championing his wife in her public career. When she sees a fellow student from law school carrying a baby instead of a briefcase, RBG knows that the difference is not in intellect or capacity, but in the mindset of their husbands: 'I married Marty… that's what divides her and me.'

For women, however privileged, who choose to be mothers, this question of how to hold and care for babies while entering 'briefcase' professions such as law and business remains a gendered challenge.

RBG's ultimately successful career on the bench does not mean that gender equality has been achieved. As the play, and her life, draw to a close, the audience sees the political ascendency of Donald Trump, his path to power undisturbed by his recorded claim to sexual abuse and blatant misogyny. For the first time, RBG is undone by anger—'[t]hat fury of mine'—and impelled to endanger her success by publicly articulating her outrage.

Despite the political changes around her, RBG retains her passionate faith in American democracy, even when it seems to be unravelling beneath the surface. This is a tension that the play alludes to: the discrimination that has been inflicted on women and on RBG specifically has been permitted within the democratic system of law and politics that she continues to champion. The slow laying down of the law over time has imprinted it with the experiences of white, male judges so that it is skewed against the perspectives of women and other marginalised groups. RBG was only the second woman appointed to the US Supreme Court in 200 years, and both of those female judges were white. If the full sum of the law is overwhelmingly decided by a single minority group, it inevitably reflects the knowledge and understanding of that group, often leaving the experiences of women and other marginalised people to be fought as 'special' cases of equality and discrimination.

As RBG demonstrates in the play, with a dissenting judgment on the legality of a strip search of a young teenage girl, law sometimes allows us a glimpse of the lack of understanding that undermines the rationality of even the most empathetic judge. While her fellow judges see no harm in the stripping and searching of a child, RBG comments '[t]hey have not been a 13 year old girl' and finds in her favour. This argument for diverse perspectives extends beyond gender. Along with many other white feminists of her era, RBG was criticised for a mixed record on race and intersectional issues, such as championing civil rights while employing few people of colour. Diverse perspectives do not guarantee equality before the law, but they broaden the experiential resources of the collective legal mind.

'The intelligence of a future day'

While another judge may have found their minority position on many key Supreme Court decisions disheartening, RBG thought of her dissenting opinions as a blueprint for future change. Her anger at injustice and inequality is soothed by the belief that, even when things go wrong in the present day, discrimination persists and politics fail, there are voices in the future that will listen and take on her blueprint.

The feminist writer Audre Lorde is often quoted as saying that 'the Master's tools will never dismantle the Master's house'. Law is one of the most powerful construction tools of contemporary life, and it continues to attract feminist activists and reformers hoping to dismantle the discriminatory systems that continue to harm women. Lorde's critique still shadows the feminist reform project. There is no doubt that RBG introduced powerful legal arguments for gender equality that have protected women's rights. Yet her unwavering belief in American democracy, and her part in it, led to her choice to remain on the Court past the time when she could have been replaced by a judge who would protect her democratic vision and equal rights legacy.

RBG's faith in democracy is underpinned by her vision of a more progressive future audience. In the play, RBG says to friend and conservative fellow judge Nico Scalia: 'I have bidden my time … I will not yield. I will be singing for justice and equality. My voice appealing to the intelligence of a future day.'

Whether one woman can change the law so that the work laid down by feminist lawyers and judges in the past can form a different kind of precedent and a more inclusive and just legal path, remains to be seen. Did RBG merely tinker at the edges of a flawed system? Will her equal rights legacy, and more, be lost? Whether her blueprint will provide the model for a new kind of legal structure depends on who is willing to take up the task. Audiences of *RBG: Of Many, One*, need to consider whether there is an 'intelligence' in the present day that will carry this equality project into the future.

Karen O'Connell

Associate Professor, Faculty of Law

University of Technology, Sydney

RBG: Of Many, One by Suzie Miller was commissioned and first produced by Sydney Theatre Company and premiered at Wharf 1 Theatre, on the lands of the Gadigal of the Eora Nation, on 3 November 2022, with the following:

RUTH BADER GINSBURG	Heather Mitchell

Director, Priscilla Jackman
Designer, David Fleischer
Lighting Designer, Alexander Berlage
Composer & Sound Designer, Paul Charlier
Assistant Director, Sharon Millerchip
Voice & Accent Coach, Jennifer White

CHARACTERS

RUTH BADER GINSBURG, at every age.

NOTES

The actor cast as Ruth plays in the given present moment of each scene unless she is reflecting within that moment or offering a legal aside.

She plays herself and all other characters.

Stage staff might be assisting if required.

A NOTE ON THE SPELLING

The playtext uses American spelling and date conventions.

TENSE

Present.

Past (relived as present).

Past (remembered).

A PLAY IN THREE PARTS

Parts One and Two contain a foundational story where various themes take us back to her at other ages and times.

Part Three is continuous, breaking the form amidst the chaos of this part.

PART ONE

1993 Sunday June 13

Ruth and Marty's place

Watergate South apartment

700 New Hampshire Road

Washington DC

Walking around the living room and watching a phone that isn't ringing.

Come on.
Ring; ring.

Put me out of misery.

Waiting.
Waiting for President Clinton to call.
To tell me I am the next judge appointed to the Supreme Court of the USA?

Waiting.
I call out to Marty.

RUTH: 'Marty, it's been hours.'

It's like a thriller,
so many secrets.
So much unknown.

Staring at this silent phone.

Come on, Mr Clinton!
Just call.

Back in time to that morning.

This morning I was up at six—and everyone knows: I hate early mornings!

Last night a wedding in Vancouver.
This morning flew back to Washington.
Airport.
Taxi,
home,
bags down, Marty made me laugh,
then right away—

Vetting team arrives.

Bernie Nussbaum from President Clinton's office leading them in.
Sets them up to go through all the folders we have laid out.
All men.
Grey suits.

Looking to find any dirt in my background.
But I have been preparing for
Mr Nussbaum—Bernie—and his team, for all my life.
They won't find anything on me.

I'm wearing navy slacks and a weekend shirt.
Bernie suggests that he and I leave.

Marty gives me a look; his eyebrows say it all:
'THIS IS IT.'

I want to change my outfit but Bernie says:

BERNIE: 'No, no it's all casual.'

RUTH: 'What?'

BERNIE: 'It's Sunday, President Clinton's day off.'

And, well
I don't want to keep him waiting,
but
navy slacks and this shirt?!

The vetting team are coo-ing around the table,
giving Marty credit for all my documents laying there in perfect chronological order.

Every single record.
All my tax files.

'Mr Ginsburg', they say, they laugh, they smile, they joke with my husband, 'you have made our job so much easier.
I guess we should not expect any less of an expert tax lawyer'.

Marty laughs along.

MARTY: 'Not me, Ruth handles all the documentation in this family.'

He smiles his beautiful smile. This is a man who can say anything and no-one ever feels chastised.

I smile too, benignly, but I know—this is part of it.

Another gender assumption.
The 'wife', even though I'm a judge, couldn't possibly organize her own documents!

They don't realize, don't even flash a look.

But I add them up,
notice every one of those little assumptions.

Not to harvest resentment.
But to really notice, to observe them all.
I file them away.
Like I file my documents.
Perfectly kept and marked.
Information there for when I need it.

'Do not invest in outrage, smile and save your time.'

Momma your words have served me well.

Back in the flat.

Marty starts making everyone coffee,
but Bernie already has me out the door …

Later.

And now, here I am nine hours later.

This day has tested my nerves.
All the testing.
All the questioning.

Waiting.

Phone ring,
please?

Come on,
I'm holding on here.

Oh and I'm still in these goddamn clothes.

1993 Sunday June 13

Washington DC

Oval Office

Back in time that Sunday. RUTH *walks into the Oval Office wearing navy slacks and a blouse.*
President Clinton stands before her behind his desk.

RUTH: 'Mr President.'

You're kidding me?
He's wearing a suit and tie.

RUTH*'s eyes watch the president stand.*

All six-feet-two inches of him!

And all five-foot-zero of me (!) is wearing my weekend travel gear!
Oh, I'm gonna kill Bernie!

Not a great start.
No time for regrets, that's what you'd say, Momma.
Smile my best smile, disarming.

CLINTON: 'Mrs Ginsburg, thank you for coming in.'

RUTH: 'Thank you so much for seeing me, President Clinton.'

She reaches forward to shake hands but can't manage.

'Yes, Mr Clinton, it was all rather amusing.
Quite the cloak-and-dagger entry.
Bernie Nussbaum snuck me in through the side door.'

CLINTON: 'I hope this morning wasn't too early for you, Mrs Ginsburg.'

RUTH: 'No, not too early at all, Mr President.'

Well that's an outright lie.

Registers her outfit.

Gotta address it.

RUTH: 'Mr President, I'm so sorry, Bernie Nussbaum assured me the attire was casual, otherwise I would never have—'

CLINTON: 'You look marvelous to me.'

RUTH: 'Thank you, Mr President.'

CLINTON: 'Ruth, please call me Bill.'

RUTH: 'Oh … Sure. Thank you … Bill.'

So … time for some small talk?

RUTH: 'Bernie Nussbaum's gone back to my apartment to join the vetting team. My husband Marty Ginsburg's going to cook them all a gourmet lunch.'

He's nodding, smiling. Such white teeth.
He remembers Marty.

CLINTON: 'Indeed, wasn't it Marty who lobbied to have your name on my shortlist?'

RUTH: 'Yes it was. That's right, he did, Mr … Bill. Oh, he's a brilliant tax lawyer, quite a different slant to my specialty.'

CLINTON: 'Shall we begin?'

RUTH: 'Yes, let's do.'

CLINTON: 'So ah, tell me about your pervading value system as a judge.'

He's leaning back in his chair. He is enjoying this.

RUTH: 'Well sir, I strongly abide by the separation of the judiciary and the executive.
The constitution can only work its magic, democracy can only be maintained,
if we never meddle in the affairs of each other.'

The president laughs.

CLINTON: 'Except for right now where I must appoint a judge and therefore, I have my nose right in the business of the judiciary!!'

Oh god, he thinks I'm preaching to him.

RUTH: 'Oh yes, of course, Mr President I fully understand … Oh, you're joking!'

He winks at me, smiling.

CLINTON: 'I've read many of your judgments, Ruth, they are quite brilliant pieces of writing.'

RUTH: 'Thank you, sir. I am honored you've read them.'

CLINTON: 'Listen. You are clearly well qualified, but tell me about yourself, Ruth?'

Huh?

RUTH: 'I'm sorry, what, sir?'

CLINTON: 'Where you are from?'

RUTH: 'Oh you want … Well, I was born in Brooklyn to a Jewish family during the depression. It certainly wasn't easy.
My mother though, Celia, she was wonderful … she talked politics and books, and in spite of being poor she was the first person to take me to the opera. It has been a great love of mine ever since.
Are you an opera lover, sir?'

CLINTON: 'No I can't say I am, Ruth.'

RUTH: 'Oh well, there's always time.'

CLINTON: 'Tell me, does Marty go with you to the opera?'

RUTH: 'Marty? Oh yes he enjoys it too.

Our apartment is right by the Kennedy Centre,
the home of the Washington National Opera.'

CLINTON: 'I think you've met my wife, Ruth, Hillary. Are you familiar with her work?'

RUTH: 'Oh yes, very much familiar. Indeed, I admire Mrs Clinton very much. She's an extremely intelligent lawyer. When your second term is served perhaps, she might even consider running for president?'

CLINTON: [*laughing*] 'Yes she is the over-achiever in our family.'

I don't quite know how to respond.

He looks right at me, it's intense, his face creases in a smile. I can see why everyone finds him so charismatic. And yet such a decent man, such a strong, committed unit with his wife.

He's talking about how Hillary had to fight at law school for everything she did.

I nod in agreement.

CLINTON: 'I admire strong women, Ruth.'

RUTH: 'Well that's a very commendable position, Mr President.'

God did I just say that out loud?

Standing up, he's standing up.

Oh, he's walking to the door …

CLINTON: 'I will be making my decision on this tonight.'

RUTH: 'Tonight. Oh. Well, if there's anything else you need … '

That smile again.

I need to ask …

She hesitates.

RUTH: ' … So, someone might call my apartment tonight then?
One way or the other?'

CLINTON: 'There will be a call one way or the other, Ruth.'

RUTH: 'Right.
Well. Thank you, Mr President.
It's been a privilege.'

What! I have to wait until tonight?

I remind myself of my momma's words.
'Patience in all things, Ruth. Patience.'

She bows and leaves the Oval Office.

1946

RUTH *is thirteen.*

RUTH: 'But I don't understand, Momma.
I can play the cello in the orchestra. I can beat all the boys in every single class at school.
I can speak Hebrew as well as all the boys.
I know more than most of them about Jewish history.
So why?
Why do they get to have a bar mitzvah?
Or rather why do the girls not get to have one?'

Celia, my mother, stops everything; looks me in the eye.

CELIA: 'Yes, it is wrong.

But hold yourself, Kiki.
Hold yourself.
See it but do not live a life of rage.
Never lose time in anger or envy.
Never raise your voice above others.

The only way to make your own life is to stay independent.
Not reliant on any man.

Be your own lady,
and your strength and independence will hold you.'

1993

Watergate South apartment

Marty opens the door.

Fills the doorway, face lights up with excitement.

He lifts me up high in the air.
This towering man and his enormous personality.

RUTH: 'Marty, stop it stop it, Marty!'

MARTY: How was it?

RUTH: 'I think it went well.
But I can't get excited yet.

She lets go, excitement.

Oh, Marty, I was in the Oval Office!'

MARTY: 'I'll bet you were wonderful.'

RUTH: 'And, Marty, the president was wearing a flash suit and tie, and I was in this!'

Marty laughs.

MARTY: 'Oh you look great, and that's not what you were there for. You're the best choice and he just needed to see for himself.'

RUTH: 'I'm not sure I said all the right things.'

Marty's telling me it's all fine.
Wants to know all about the Oval Office, what it was like.

But my anxiety is taking over.

Marty is making tea, I follow him around.

RUTH: 'I did give my usual speech about separation of powers
… But maybe he was insulted by that?'

MARTY: 'Come on, drink your tea, you would have impressed him no end—when does he decide?'

RUTH: 'Oh, Marty, I can't drink tea right now. I'm all butterflies and nervousness. He said tonight. But does that start at five p.m.? Shall I ask Bernie?'

She walks around the apartment.

Marty puts on a radio channel playing opera.
He knows me so well.
This man, this love of mine.

RUTH: 'Puccini!'

I think of my mother.
She feels so close today.

Music plays on the radio—'The Stars are Shining' from the opera Tosca.

Heather Mitchell in Sydney Theatre Company's RBG: Of Many, One*, 2023 (Photo: Prudence Upton)*

1948

RUTH *is sixteen.*

Opera playing, but not on the radio, it is increasingly as if there is an opera surrounding her.

For my sixteenth birthday my parents buy me an opera ticket.
It's expensive.
I know much is sacrificed to pay for it.
I cherish it. Place it in my jewelry box until the day arrives.

Sixteen is delightful,
I have a few interested young men, all smart and fun.
I enjoy being told I am beautiful;
my parents are wary.

CELIA: 'Ruth, schoolwork must always come first.'

RUTH: 'Of course it does, Momma.'

I take the subway into the city with my mother.
On the train in she takes her beloved brooch from her own coat,
pins this precious sparkling piece onto my lapel.
It's done in silence; for this special day.

I must go into the opera house matinee alone.
Only one ticket.
My mother will wait outside until the end.

I make my way to my seat.
The excitement, the grandness of it all.

The opera song volume increases.

And then,
in the middle of a perfectly ordinary afternoon,
I am transported.
I am the notes.

It's overwhelming. I am holding my breath.

Then the aria plays at full volume—'The Stars Are Shining'.

It's exquisite.

An aria is upon me:

'And the stars were shining and the earth was centered.'

Puccini is teaching me about love.

RUTH *is profoundly moved.*

The aria lifts me beyond myself,
beyond my studies, beyond striving.
Beyond the difficulties of life.
Beyond anxiety. Beyond fear.
And I soar.

Something inside me is deeply connected to another world.
I am connected to a deep well of purity,
to the vulnerability of being human.

I realize my cheeks are wet
to the bone.

I want to sing opera—use my voice.
I want to be up on a stage singing to the world
of hardship and pain.
Of love and desire.
Of humanity.

I want to breathe in this life,
and reach great heights.

Return to:

1993 Sunday June 13

Washington DC

Later, 6 p.m.
The phone rings.

I freeze,

I pick up the phone.

Marty's leaning over me,
trying to hear what's being said.

RUTH: 'Hello. Hello.
Yes, this is Justice Ginsburg
Oh, hello, Bernie.
[*To Marty*] This is not the call.'

Marty slumps.

RUTH: 'Oh, I see
No, no of course.'

I cover the phone.

RUTH: [*to Marty*] 'The president has friends over and they're watching a basketball game together!
What is this game, Marty?'

Marty rushes to the other room.
Turns on the game.

RUTH: [*on phone*] 'Oh okay, well thank you, Bernie.'

She hangs up.

Marty calls out something about Basketball Finals,
the Chicago Bulls and the Phoenix Suns.

MARTY: 'The president played college basketball.
Was very good at it too.'

But I am not listening, I don't care whether the president was good at college sport,
I care about what decision he made today.
And why the wait?

Does he have doubts?

MARTY: 'I think his team is winning.'

RUTH: 'Do you think that's a good sign? Yes?'

Calm, breathe, wait.

It occurs to me
Who the hell does the president even support? The Bulls or the Suns?
If he loses will he just go to bed and not call?

MARTY: 'It's actually a good game,
and there's a bit to go yet, Kiki.'

1950

This House of Grief

Kiki. My name to my momma, to my family.

Me, Kiki, my mother's second daughter.
Loved by an older sister I was never old enough to remember,
other than through my mother's stories.

I grew up in a house of grief, air thick with loss.
It was my older sister who playfully renamed me.

[*Imitates a six-year-old girl*] 'She kicks her legs all day, Momma, we should call her "Kiki".'

A six-year-old sister Marilyn lives with me forever.
In the pet name she bestowed upon me before her tragic death.

And now,
I'm eighteen and tomorrow is my graduation.
A chair in the auditorium of the James Madison High School Hall,
with my formal name on it: Joan Ruth Bader.
But without you there, Momma,
I will not go to the ceremony.
This house is engulfed in grief again.
Same smell, same silence, same heaviness.
Yet this time I am not peering in, I'm here at the center of it.
A tsunami of gut-wrenching hurt.
My mother is dying.
The pain settles like a mist, a weight, an unbearable emptiness.

My father is weeping and between us is only space.

Space that is her. My momma. My Celia. My light.

Waiting for years for me to get to this point.
She waited,
through her agonizing illness she waited.
Till I received my university offer, my scholarship, she waited.

All that time marking time, trying to stay with me.

Beat.

My cheek close against yours, breathing each other in.
Silently counting down the days, the hours, the minutes.
Every one of them a desperate gift.

When you slip away
your dreams for me
becoming mine to action.

I leave soon for Cornell.
The university my mother dreamed of
for herself.
Cornell,
our one joint dream.

My father and aunt are telling me that we need to find ten men to start the prayers for my mother.
But I am not to be counted amongst the ten mourners.

I do not count for the prayers?
I do not count because I am NOT a man.

And it is not right.

Beat.

And I'm trying, Momma.
Trying to hold it together for you,
to not resent, to not waste my mind or my time.
But I do resent it, Momma,
I am angry.

I should be the one leading your Minyan,
Your Kiki, your Ruth.
Not those strange men they are rounding up who didn't even know you.

I love my Jewish culture, the gentle intelligence of it
but not this part,
not the part that excludes me, because of my sex, from taking my rightful position.

1951

Cornell

It's exciting here.
Cornell.

Professor Nabokov tells me:
You can [*imitating him*] 'paint pictures with words'.
And I love that.

It's so romantic.
And it makes sense.
Words, music, opera: my ways of making sense of it all.
It excites me.

Spellbinding lessons.
Professor Nabokov,
his wife Vera sitting up the back and shaking her head
whenever he plays the showman.

Which he does a lot.
So there is a lot of head-shaking!

McCarthyism raises its ugly head.
Academics from Cornell are called to the House of Un-American activities.

Professor Cushman wants me to understand
civil liberties, constitutional rights.
He thinks I should consider going to law school.

MR CUSHMAN: 'With the law
You can change things,
with words.'

Law School?
ME!

It feels right.

But in the meantime, there is a blind date to go on.

Marty Ginsburg is a year ahead of me.
He is everything I am not.
Tall,
hilarious,
filled with super confidence.
And the only guy I know on campus with a car!

He is also the only boy I ever knew who cared that I had a brain.

Marty Ginsburg leans in to kiss me
and in that moment
everything is certain.
He is the only man I ever love
I am the only woman he will love.

Marty changes his subjects to do the same ones as me,
and
to fit in with his ridiculous golfing fanaticism!

He does constitutional law with me, and I encourage him to go to Harvard Law School instead of Business School.

RUTH: [*to Marty*] 'For god's sake, Harvard Business School still doesn't take women students!'

Marty laughs but he strongly agrees with my outrage.

Marty goes to Harvard Law School ahead of me,
while I finish my year at Cornell.

Joan Bruder, my dear friend at Cornell, is marrying a guy who is also at Harvard Law School.

But her parents say now she's getting married, they will no longer pay the university fees for her degree.
She must leave without graduating.

One by one the women fall aside.

RUTH *makes a face.*

After I graduate Cornell,
Marty goes down on one knee.

On the day of our wedding, Marty's mum, Evelyn, who I adore, takes me aside.
She hands me a tiny box.

My new mother-in-law tells me that:

EVELYN: 'Inside this box is the secret to a happy marriage.'

Intrigued I gently unlatch the box.
Curiosity overwhelms me.

I peer down earnestly at a pair of …

ear plugs?
And Marty's mother says:

EVELYN: 'It helps sometimes to be a little deaf, dear.'

We both burst out laughing.

Return to:

1993 Sunday June 13

Watergate South apartment

Washington DC

Marty's yelling.

MARTY: 'The game's going into its SECOND overtime!'

Oh, I don't even care who's winning.

And Marty's all involved in the game now.

This is pure torture!

I have
been waiting for HOURS for a man who is watching a basketball final to decide whether I get to step up onto the Supreme Court of the United State of America.

There is so much riding on this.

But Marty is yelling.

MARTY: 'The Bulls are losing.'

RUTH: 'Is that a bad sign?'

MARTY: 'It's Clinton's team.'

That's bad.

1956

Harvard

The Dean of Harvard Law School is looking at all of us,
around the dinner table.

We have been heralded by him,
all nine of us.

The only nine women who have been accepted into Law at Harvard, in a cohort of five hundred.

He has invited each of us here
to ask us 'Why you think you have the right to take up a space at law school
instead of a man?'

I know what I want to say.
I light up a cigarette,
as the first woman student is called upon.

WOMAN 1: 'Well, sir, I was first in my undergraduate year,
and my professor suggested I should apply.'

The dean is unmoved.
In my belly the fight is on.

Why are we asked to do this?
We have all sat our LSATS,
we have earned our places here at Harvard. Proven ourselves.

Another woman is responding to the question.
She has to make her answer palatable.

WOMAN 2: 'My place in law school is to
fulfil my father's dream
of having a lawyer in the family.'

I'm juggling the ashtray in my lap
dressed up like all the others.

Fuming on the inside.
But I try not to hear the scorn in the dean's voice,
I try to focus on why I am here.

Drag on the cigarette,
feel the heady smoke in my bloodstream.

I think about what my mother Celia would expect me to say,
what Marty would laugh at.

Hold in the outrage.
Bide my time.
Keep them happy.
Play the game.

I have a flash of last night's study session with my beautiful husband,
listless in his hospital bed.

How did this happen? My beloved Marty.
Marty is sick, testicular cancer. So desperately ill.

He reminds me of my need to finish this degree, in case … in case he doesn't make it … but I cannot think like that!

Because we have our beautiful baby girl Jane now.
Our bonny daughter, and she needs us both.

After class and feeding Jane.
I come to the hospital.
Every evening.
Bring Marty the law notes from his peers;
talk them through with him so he won't lose his graduation date.
He's too weak to write, so he dictates to me between midnight and two a.m.,
I then do my own study;
learn to live on two hours' sleep.
And to hope.
I don't believe in prayer these days,
but hope.
I do believe in hoping,
and working.
Because together that keeps my mind occupied.

My turn.
All eyes are upon me,
all eight sets of women's eyes.
And the dean,
whose wife has left the room to check on the next serving.

I want to say: 'I'm here at Harvard because *Brown versus the Board of Education* matters to me—the rights to non-segregated schools.
It's a recent case that has inspired me about equality and rights,
run by a lawyer I very much admire, Thurgood Marshall.'
I want to say: 'I WANT TO BE THE THURGOOD MARSHALL for women.
To fight for women's equality.'
But that is not what I say.
I pull myself up and I follow the advice of my mother.
'Be strategic. Be careful, smile. Be a laaaady.'

I, Ruth Bader Ginsburg, the smartest student in the room
hear myself say:

RUTH: 'I guess I must study law so that I can talk to my husband about his work.'

I was being ironic, but … no-one is smiling.

Shame immediately follows.
I stub out my cigarette,
a little too hard.
The tiny ashtray slips, and ash goes everywhere.
On my hands,
on my skirt,
and a dirty mark on the pristine carpet,
that the dean's wife is rushing to clean just as it hits the ground.
Oh god.

Thank god I have already been given my place here at Harvard Law School!

Return to:

1993 Sunday June 13

Watergate South apartment

Washington DC

With a roar, the game is over.

Marty calls out:

MARTY: 'Three hours! This is one of the longest basketball game finals in history.'

Great, so the game makes history!

Marty is trying to keep optimistic.

RUTH: 'Maybe he is seeing his friends out?'

I think: 'Only a man could possibly think basketball is more important than the future of the Supreme Court.'

1960s and 1970s

Marty is well,
his cancer is gone,
Jane is bonny.

Marty finishes law school and applies for jobs!

But!!
Here in Boston the anti-Semitism amongst top law firms shocks us both.
There are no jobs for Marty, brilliant Marty.

Then suddenly a job at Weil, Gotshal and Manges in New York City. Brilliant news!
We plan our move
but the Dean of Law at Harvard tells me: 'No, you may not complete your Harvard degree unless you remain in Boston.' Yep, him again!

So I transfer to Columbia University, New York City. So long Harvard!

And then
Marty and I are so blessed because
despite all the odds of Marty's cancer,
I am pregnant again,
and darling James, our miracle baby, is born.
Our family is complete.

1959, my graduation day
Columbia University.
As I collect my degree I hear a small girl's voice
ring out over the quiet formality. It's Jane.

'That's my mommy.'

A ripple in the auditorium,
My mouth a wide, wide smile.

The future looks so rosy.

I've topped the year.

There's nothing stopping me now.
I heartily apply for law jobs.

THEN:

Letters from different voices.

LETTER: 'Dear Mrs Ginsburg
We do not hire women lawyers.'

LETTER: 'Dear Mrs Ginsburg
We have no idea why any woman would want to work in a man's job.'

LETTER: 'Dear Mrs Ginsburg
I'm afraid our firm would not fare well in our wives' opinions if we hired women in legal roles. We are sure your husband would agree with us on this matter.'

My degree.
First in class.
And now … Dead end.

I have three strikes:
I'm a woman.
I'm a mother.
And I'm Jewish.

Yet there are men who are my allies.

There's Professor Cushman,
and Nabokov from Cornell.

And then
Professor Gunther from Columbia Law School.
He calls a New York judge he knows.
The judge is not convinced—'A woman, who has children?!'

But Professor Gunther insists.

Begrudgingly the judge takes me on—I work so damn hard he never regrets it.

The other man who's my ally is Marty,
my secret weapon.

He believes in sharing the raising of our children.
And this changes everything.
He cooks every meal, not just because I am a lousy cook!
And we take turns to do the cleaning.

I run into
a friend from Harvard. She's smart.
I tell her I'm clerking, lecturing at law school and
starting to run cases, interesting cases.

She looks at me,

FRIEND: 'I knew you were smart.

Super smart.
But so was I, wasn't I?'

I nod.

She's juggling her baby
and a baby's bottle.
I'm juggling a brief
on my way to court.

FRIEND: 'Why? Why not me?' she says

I whisper softly.

RUTH: 'It's just … I married Marty.'

I say this with compassion
because I know that's what divides her and me.

She nods, tears in her eyes.

That night I go home and as Marty is cooking dinner
chatting to Jane and James.
I walk over to him.
I hold him close.
He laughs.
Delighted!

RUTH: 'Thank you.'

I say,
heartfelt.

He smiles.

MARTY: 'You haven't tasted it yet'

1970s

It begins …

After my work with the judge, the 1970s throws up a medley of cases.

I start working at the American Civil Liberties Union,
with an interest in justice for women.

AND it all begins with
Charles Moritz.

Marty throws a tax article on my desk.

MARTY: 'Read it.'

RUTH: 'I don't read tax cases.'

And this one.
Wow.
This one is a zinger.

Sure, it's about a man,
but what better way to get the men to see the injustice.

Charles Moritz.
Loves his mom
he wants to care for her in her old age.
But because he is an unmarried man
he cannot have the tax deduction!

On the basis of his sex, Charles Moritz is being treated differently.
His rights under the Constitution's Fourteenth Amendment that 'all are equal before the law'
are being breached.

Marty and I prepare court submissions!

The legal team come over
Marty cooks his usual gourmet meals
I prepare the briefs
Marty yelling tax cases to check out.
We take it to court,
and … Charles Moritz wins!
He gets his tax benefits.

We did it
I can feel the buzz.
This one case,
it changed the law!

I need to find another case to do this again!

Next,
Reed versus Reed.
Mrs Reed is divorced.
Her ex-husband insisted their son live with him.
But the boy hated it, he was frightened.
Mrs Reed could do nothing.
Then her poor boy takes his own life.

And the law dares to say to her, 'You are not entitled to his estate, not to any of his things
because only a man can take possession of an estate.'

BUT Mrs Reed decides to fight.

For the first time as a lawyer
I am standing up in the Supreme Court
all five feet of me
arguing before the highest judges in the land.

RUTH: 'The Fourteenth Amendment of the constitution does not allow discrimination on the basis of sex.'

And …
we win!!!!

Mrs Reed's loss is unfathomable
but she has done a big thing.

This is a step towards equality.

Me!
I can do this!
I can fight for women, all women.
By arguing each individual case of discrimination 'on the basis of sex'.

Marty's secretary Lorna types up all my briefs.
I visit Marty's office.

LORNA: 'Oh, Mrs Ginsburg! I had no idea it was you writing all of these.
I'm typing all these briefs and articles for you and the word "sex", "sex", "sex" is on every page.
Don't you do know that those nine men on the Supreme Court they hear that word, and their first association is not what you want them to be thinking. Why don't you use the word gender? It is a grammatical term and it will ward off any distracting associations.'

She's right!

From now on gender discrimination it is.

Frontiero versus Richardson.

Sharron Frontiero.
Member of the military.
Where all the men can claim living benefits for their spouses
but she cannot.

RUTH *in court.*

RUTH: 'Your Honors, why would our constitution allow for soldiers to receive living benefits for their spouses but then deny a particular soldier, because of their gender, that same right?
Such rules keep women in a place inferior to that occupied by men in our society. It is inconsistent and must not be allowed.'

We …

She waits.

win!!!

Oh my, this is my special skill.

1978 Duren versus Missouri.
Women are allowed to be excused from juries due to home duties!

I argue in court:

RUTH: 'This is one of those double-edged discriminations characteristic of the law—that chivalrous gentlemen, sitting in an all-male chamber, misconceive as a favor to the "ladies", that they are too preoccupied with home and children and should therefore be spared the civic duty of serving on a jury.
The Constitution of the United States of America cannot tolerate a system where women are not judged by their own peers.'

This is a big one.
Women on juries means they get to judge.
We … win!

Incremental change. Step by step.

One win at a time.
Each plotted as part of the bigger picture.

This is it.
I have found my calling in life,
and in LAW.

THEN
in 1973 there's a landmark abortion case being heard before the Supreme Court.

Roe versus Wade.

It's not my case but I follow it closely of course.

Everyone celebrates a big win.
But … HANG ON.

The court held that the right to abortion rests on the right to privacy between a woman and her doctor.
It isn't strong enough.

The win in Roe versus Wade isn't really about the women's choice, it's about the doctor's freedom to practice. The tall doctor and the little woman. It isn't woman-centred, it is physician-centred.

I speak up.

RUTH: 'I believe that the Court got it wrong on abortion rights, it's not secure enough.
Whether or not to bear a child is central to a woman's life, to her well-being and dignity.
It is a decision that she must make for herself.
When Government controls that decision for her, she is being treated less than a fully adult human responsible for her own choices.'

But …
everyone thinks because I criticized the decision I am not celebrating abortion rights!!

No. No!
I'm saying the court failed to make abortion
a watertight right.
I'm warning that one day abortion rights can be overturned!

I am not popular for speaking out.
But I must use my voice
even when I am in the minority.
Perhaps even …
Especially when I am in the minority.

Return to:

1993 Sunday June 13

Watergate South apartment

Washington DC

The phone rings loudly.

I hesitate.
What if … ?

What will I tell my granddaughter?
That we nearly made it?

I'm scared.

Marty is in his pajamas
about to spring.

I pick up the phone before he can.
It's all crackly.

RUTH: 'Hello, Mr President?
[*To Marty*] He hung up!'

Dial tone.

Marty and I wait in utter silence,
I can't look at him.

Phone ring.

RUTH: 'Hello?
Hello?
[*To Marty*] It's a terrible connection.'

Then I hear the forty-second President of the United States of America say to me:

CLINTON: 'If I'm going to propose, we might as well have a good line.'

RUTH: [*to Marty*] 'Is he cracking a joke?'

She awkwardly laughs.

CLINTON: 'Hang up I'll call ya right back.'

RUTH: 'Marty, I am so over this comedy of errors.

Phone rings and she jumps right onto it.

Hello.'

And I hear
loud and clear
President Bill Clinton word for word:

CLINTON: 'I'm going to ask you tomorrow, in the Rose Garden at the White House, to accept a position as one of the nine judges on the Supreme Court of the United State of America.'

Marty is dancing around; he sees my face.
I must be beaming because he laughs.

RUTH: [*to Clinton, down the line*] 'Thank you, Mr President. I must write my speech.'

CLINTON: 'Ruth, might I say, write something from the heart and the mind.'

RUTH: 'Thank you, Mr President.'

RUTH *hangs up the phone.*

Marty pops some champagne.

MARTY: 'You are now one of the nine judges on the Supreme Court—and only the second woman. Well done Kiki!'

We hug.

I go to my cupboard.

I take out the jacket that I dreamt of wearing if I was asked to take up the position.
I pin my mother's brooch to the lapel.
Left-hand side, over my heart.

And in this moment, I know, my life is changed forever.

TRANSITION BETWEEN PARTS ONE AND TWO

PART TWO

2013 Monday July 1

Washington DC, Kennedy Centre at the Opera

The finale of the opera Tristan and Isolde *starts softly then builds and builds.*

RUTH *listens with her eyes closed.*

Some time passes as the music is all about us. It continues throughout the scene.

Oh Marty, I wish you were still here on this earth with me.

Tristan and Isolde.
A love story.

But not nearly a match for ours.

I move in my seat beside Nino. My dear friend.

Who buoys me in these years after Marty's death.

Tomorrow, and for the second time in my life,
I will meet with a president at the White House. Ten years since I was last there.

SCALIA: 'Kiki, tomorrow is Obama. But tonight you need to be here with the music.'

Justice Nino Scalia.
My colleague
and unlikely friend.

His right-wing conservative politics
starkly in contrast with mine.
Yet a mind to behold,
as piercing as a Wagner opera.
A hot knife through butter.
My dear Nino
we are bound
never to agree.

And yet,
like no-one else
he makes me better.
This man who is smarter than all the others
sets out to slice my words apart

and in doing so prepares me for the voice of opposition.

RUTH: 'I believe in listening to those I disagree with and finding areas to build together. Inching us all closer to equality.'

The music.
I let myself go.
I feel myself meld with a magical soprano voice.

Every bar of music touches me on a cellular level. Takes me with it.

When the curtain falls
Nino leans closer.
He has seen my tears.

SCALIA: 'Kiki, in court you are tough
but look at you, my friend,
here you are a pussycat.'

She laughs.

I have bidden my time
and tomorrow when I lunch with this new president at the White House.
I will not yield.
I will be singing
for justice and equality.
My voice appealing to the intelligence of a future day.

1994

Supreme Court of the United States of America Building

Peter, my court assistant, pops his head.

PETER: 'Justice Ginsburg.
There are five little girls outside the court with their mothers.'

RUTH: 'Oh yes.
It's Clara's third birthday.
Please show them in.
And I have a cake in the kitchen with three candles,
when you hear loud singing, can you bring it in please?

Come on, Clara.
Hello, girls.
I am Clara's granny.
Her bubbie.

Why don't you each take a seat up there on one of those nine chairs.
That's right.
Can you see over the bench there, dear?
Now you're all judges.

And maybe one day you might like to come and work here too.
Because you know what?
This is a place for all American people.

For a long time, only boys could come here to talk about things.
But that wasn't fair. Was it? No.
So now there are two grannies here. Me and Justice Sandra O'Connor and we are good friends.
Because girls belong in all the places where decisions are being made.'

1996

It's tense in the judge's discussion room.

US versus VMI

Women are denied entry to the Virginia Military Institute.
The Constitution is clear,
we must all be equal before the law.

This case is a chance to give women equal rights!
Inside I am euphoric.
This is my mission,
this case could change everything!
And I am part of it.

All the judges are animated, even Chief Justice Rehnquist is prepared to strike down this law. Good for him.

Justice Sandra O'Connor, the only other female judge, posits:

O'CONNOR: 'We could argue that women have the right to equal protection under the Fourteenth.'

Justice Nino Scalia disagrees.

SCALIA: 'Our constitution should not be read to create a law where there is none.'

Chief Justice Rehnquist decides that Nino will write the one judgment in dissent.
He turns to Sandra O'Connor and suggests that she write the majority judgment.

JUDGE: 'This will be a major precedent for equality.'

Sandra shakes her head.

SANDRA: 'This should be Ruth's.'

Sandra, the first woman on the bench, a Republican,
she's reaching out to me
beyond the partisan divide.
Beyond all our differences

with welcoming arms.

All eyes are upon me,
I'm ready,
I have never been so excited,
but my face—a mask!

I argue my point:

RUTH: 'I see the constitution as a living document that calls for equality before the law.'

They all nod in agreement.
Except Justice Nino Scalia that is.
He's adamant that the constitution
makes no reference to equality on the basis of gender.
He sees our constitution as a dead document without contemporary context.

Before Nino heads off for a weekend trip away
he throws onto my desk a draft of his minority dissent judgment.

Sharp,
focused arguments against my own position.
Beautiful sentences.

Frighteningly intelligent.

And a gift,
because it allows me to hone in on exactly what I need to refute.
I write all night.

… and I read out
my majority judgment in court.
My words.
My voice.

RUTH, *in court.*

RUTH: [*to Judge*] While it might be that many women.
Myself, my daughter, you or yours
might not want to attend the Virginia Military Institute
as well your sons might choose not to.
It stands that there are women who do want to attend.
And those women must have that right.
This finding effectively strikes down any law which, denies to women, simply because they are women, full citizenship stature—equal opportunity to aspire, achieve, participate in and contribute to society.'

BINGO.

This case is a zinger!

And this is the beginning!
I look over to Nino, Justice Scalia.
He smiles.
At me.
My heart's pounding,
I touch my mother's brooch
and smile back.

Return to:

2013 Monday July 1

Washington DC

RUTH *is dressed in a fabulous suit.*

I'm ushered into the White House
This time no secret side entry on a Sunday.
Right through the front doors.

I walk down the hallway towards the President's Oval Office
flanked by aides and security.
This time I like what I'm wearing!

Walk past portraits of all those who had once sat here before him.

All those men.
All those white men.

I walk once more into the Oval Office.

And there stands:
President Obama.

Sharply dressed.
Slimline.
Intelligent smile.

Wise eyes.

He invites me to take lunch with him.

We move towards a tastefully decorated dining room.

Make chat.

He asks me about my health,
I bristle.

1999

It's 1999 when I get my diagnosis.
I am silent.
I focus on the lapel of the white coat behind the desk,
Jewish doctor, not much younger than me.
Kindly face, mouth moving.

Justice Sandra O'Connor,
my sister on the bench,

gives me advice.

O'CONNOR: 'Schedule your chemo for Fridays
so you will be okay by Monday and back at work.'

Brilliant advice it turns out.
I never miss a court sitting.

I didn't know she had suffered breast cancer.
Her recovery
Marty's recovery
gives me hope against my mother Celia's early death.

From one hundred pounds I lose pound after pound,
Marty tempts me with spoonfuls of home-made chicken soup.
But work continues.
I can't be seen as weak,
vulnerable.

I wake one night in a sweat,
death looms at three a.m.
I'm frightened,

I don't want my children to live
in a house of grief.

I have so much to do,
I feel strong arms about me,
Marty's eyes looking right into me.

He knows.
He has been here.
This despair.
Cancer,
yet again in our lives.

MARTY: 'You're strong,'

he says,

MARTY: 'stronger than anyone I have ever known.'

Return to:

2013 Monday July 1

Washington DC

A gentleman in a dinner suit fills my glass.
Sparkling water with a slice of lime.

RUTH: 'Thank you.'

Mr President has the same.

We both know why I am here,
but he can't find the right way in.

Yet.

He will have no help from me.

It is his dance around the law that must be done. Not mine.

He is the first African-American man in office.
Smart,
thoughtful.

Careful.
I like that about him.

Light years ahead of his Bush predecessor. Obama is intelligent while Bush was a fool the likes of which I can't imagine we shall ever see in the White House again, thank goodness!

But it is precisely because of this young president's care and intelligence, that I must remain on guard.

2000

Fireworks.
Happy New Year! A new millennium. It is the year 2000. My cancer is in remission.
Life is precious.
The sun has come out and

and …
another two white men
are running for President.
Bush or Gore (!).

The election is being counted when there is a snag in Florida
and all hell breaks out.
Bush is declaring victory.
It makes its way up to my court.
The Supreme Court.
The conservative judges agree with Bush's case. I am in the
minority.
The recount is stopped,

and,
just like that
Bush becomes the next President of the United States.

I never dreamed that this country would decide the presidency before
it was certain the voting was fair.
But yes this man is in office.

And for me, something has shifted.
Something is very clear.

If I am to be so often in the minority of this group of judges
then I must find a way to make sure that my dissenting judgments, my voice, my ideas
really matter.

Return to:

2013 Monday July 1

Washington DC

White House

French onion soup as a starter.
I delicately dab my napkin on my lips.

Delicious.
We
both agree.
Our plates are taken away.
But not the massive elephant
sitting on the table between us.

I ask about his girls.
His daughters.
He asks about my grandchildren.

Is this pointed?
Is he talking about the relative ages of us both?

He tells me how much he admired my judgment in the Ledbetter case.

I tell him how excited I was when he took my judgment,
despite it being a dissent, a minority judgment, and presented it to Congress,
and enacted it as law.

OBAMA: 'There was no way that brilliant judgment of yours on Ledbetter was not going to influence congress. It gave me exactly what I needed to draft into law equal pay despite gender as the law of the nation.'

[*Cynical*] He is flattering me.

2007

It's 2007 and I am hitting my stride

The Lilly Ledbetter case comes to court.
She is the top performer at Goodyear Tires
yet consistently paid less than her male counterparts over the entire nineteen years she works as a manager for them in Alabama.
She is not letting them get away with it and
sues for repayment of equal pay.
She loses,
but then appeals all the way
to our court, the Supreme Court.

Chief Justice Roberts says: 'No, this appeal cannot be upheld. If this case won, it would open the floodgates to all other minorities.'

I'm furious, I ask Roberts if I can write the dissent judgment.
He's pleased I want to, there's no-one else jumping up for it, and I work night and day to demolish what the majority write.

Lilly Ledbetter had lost her case but my words are there in my dissent.

I was not part of the majority but I work as hard on this dissent judgment as if I were. Because one day it might be read.
The fairness of my argument, that women have the right to be paid the same amount as men when they do the same work, will be understood—and made law of the land.

Return to:

2013 Monday July 1

Washington DC

When the main meal arrives
it is too big for me.

And my stomach is churning in anticipation of the discussion to follow.

President Obama eats.

RUTH: [*to Obama*] 'The beauty of a democracy is exactly Ledbetter in action.
Is it not?'

Obama nods.

The smallest purse of his lips.

We are both doing a complex dance about the issue.

I begin again.

RUTH: 'The judiciary must never tell Congress what to do.
And although, Mr President, you took my dissent judgment in Ledbetter and drafted it into law, you only did this because you and your team believed it fair.
I was, of course, thrilled my dissenting voice was heard.
But I would never ask you to change the law, Mr President,
that would be a breach of democracy itself.
For me to interfere with how you run your office.

The separation of President and Congress from the Judiciary is one of the pillars of the United States democratic system.
We must never interfere or tell each other what to do.
We are each other's checks and balances to guard against a rogue court or a rogue president.'

He's smiling ever so slightly.

I am not eating my chicken breast,
despite the delicious sauce splashed delicately upon it.

The broccolini is untouched.

The president neatly lies down his fork.

OBAMA: 'This is delicate for me, Justice Ginsburg.'

I say nothing.

OBAMA: 'I am well into my second and final term.'

I say nothing.

OBAMA: 'Midterms are almost upon us.'

I say nothing.
I know what lies beneath this.
I hear her voice, Celia's, my mother's: 'Hold yourself, Kiki.
Hold yourself.'

But a fire burns in my belly
and for the first time since
I wanted to lead prayers at my mother's Minyan.

I let a glimpse of my fury emerges.

RUTH: 'Of course, I know, Mr President, exactly what this "delicate" conversation is about.'

OBAMA: 'I do not doubt that for a moment, Ruth.'

Ruth?
He's dropped the formality.

RUTH: 'I am a woman in a position of power.
A woman amongst a majority of men.
But that is not the issue here.
I am the oldest serving Justice on the Court.

And like every judge ever to serve on that court,
the law says that as long as I am fit and able I am to continue to serve.
There has been no change to that law as far as I know.'

He looks at me
Is he afraid to speak?
No, he is strategically letting me voice the unsayable.

RUTH: 'I understand that before this midterm election
where you are bound to lose Senate seats
that you would like to appoint a younger judge onto the Supreme Court
and in that way you will have your voice in that court going forward.'

He doesn't move.

RUTH: 'And you are talking to me
to question whether I would retire in order to serve that purpose?'

OBAMA: 'I would never ask you to serve my purpose, Ruth, I am interested only in whether you have considered retiring.'

I am silent.

He is silent.

Then I dare to ask:

RUTH: 'Why?'

He is in a corner,
there is nowhere to go.
He must state that he wants me out so his legacy will live on.
That if I die in office after midterms
and if there is a change of government
that I could be replaced with a conservative judge.
And he is trying to make sure he safeguards the court against this.

Against my death.
But this is NOT what democracy envisions.

I place my knife and fork neatly together on my uneaten plate of food
and a waiter comes to collect both of our plates

Clatter of plates
clatter of cutlery
cut between the president and myself
utter silence reigns.

2009

On an ordinary day in 2009 I am diagnosed with another cancer: this time pancreatic.
Soon after Marty's cancer returns.

We shall fight it together.
With love and family and our combined strength.
Our children, grandchildren.

My granddaughter Clara is only eighteen years old; I want to leave her in a more equitable world.
There is so much I still need to do.

So many rights that women are yet to be granted!

In court there is an appeal case: a thirteen-year-old girl is stripped to her underwear
and undergoes a body search for prescription-strength painkillers. School officials then shook out her bra, stretched out the top of her pants and shook them out.

Justice Breyer asks: 'What's the big deal? Children change every day for the gym at school.'
The male judges are nodding, quizzical. Jokes being cracked, one of them even laughs.

But I am clear.

RUTH: 'None of you has lived experience as a
thirteen-year-old girl.
The girl gave her account as embarrassing, frightening and humiliating.
And I would add abusive.'

Silence.

The laughing is over.
Maybe now they see why having a woman on the bench is so important.

I am sometimes asked: 'When will there be enough women on the Supreme Court?' and I say: 'When there are nine.'

She laughs cheekily.

Return to:

2013 Monday July 1

Washington DC

OBAMA: 'A green tea please.'

Obama is ordering tea.

He thinks, then he speaks.

OBAMA: 'Of course, should you retire,
I would want to reassure you that it would be a woman.
Any judge I appoint.'

This is supposed to placate me.

RUTH: 'Your desired replacement for me?'

He lets the question answer itself.

RUTH: 'I have no intention of dying, Mr President.'

He hurries in.

OBAMA: 'I would hope not, Ruth,
I was just interested in what your next move might be?'

RUTH: 'Mr President as you know,
like yourself,
I hold the institution of democracy in the highest regard.

And I know you have taken my dissent in Ledbetter and made it law.

But,
that decision was entirely YOUR decision.
I have never asked you,
nor invited you to lunch, to suggest you do so.'

He is uncomfortable.

OBAMA: 'I hope you know
I would never ever assume to influence you, Justice Ginsburg.'

RUTH: 'Oh I know, Mr President.
Democracy, and I know you agree with me on this, is about the voracity of its institutions.

They are separated and can speak out without being leant upon by each other.

It is only this that allows us both to uphold the most important of all rules.
The Rule of Law.
Everyone is entitled to fairness,
no-one is above the law,
not even you or I, Mr President.

RUTH *smiles a benevolent smile.*

It would be a folly to squander this for short-term legacies and future-proofing of the courts.'

OBAMA: 'But tell me, what of your legacy, Justice Ginsburg?'

I falter.
He's smart,
knows my Achilles.

I inwardly shudder at all the work I have done in the courts being undone by a future right-wing court.

RUTH: 'Well, Mr President, judges unlike presidents are appointed for life.
Even if the next president comes in and appoints Supreme Court judges neither of us would approve of,
that is our great democracy in action.

In my experience judges are collegiate,
their minds can work together beyond party lines.'

The president considers me.

RUTH: 'And, Mr President,
I believe I have much work to do.
My dissenting judgments have only just begun.

They are letters written to the future.

Presidents might lay down train tracks but so too do judges.
Presidents might be looking to the next government term,
But judges are writing to those yet to be born.

I owe you a great gratitude, Mr President.
Because it was you who
showed me through your action on Ledbetter,
that dissent judgments have a place,
and they can effect great change.

I will dedicate myself to making sure my dissents speak with humanity and clarity.'

His eyes glimmer.
We are similar he and I.
We both know it.

RUTH: 'And, Mr President,
as your second (and final) term comes to its close
I am optimistic
and quietly confident
that we will see the first female President of the United States.

I will just have to stay alive until then, will I not, Mr President?'

He smiles right at me.

Defeated.

Then charmingly:

OBAMA: 'I hope you live a lot longer than that, Justice Ginsburg.'

2010

I am recovered from my pancreatic cancer.

But Marty is sicker and sicker,
his cancer has metastasized.

I spend every spare moment I can with him.

I stand to leave his hospital room this afternoon,
lean in and kiss his brow.
Our eyes meet and we both smile without words.

Beat.

Today out of the blue I find in my purse a letter he has written from his hospital bed.

I'm confused.

Marty. I'm seeing you tonight!
You old softy.

I open the envelope licked with his own dear mouth.

Unfold the letter as I put the kettle on to boil.

MARTY: 'My dearest Ruth,
setting aside our parents, kids, their kids—you are the only person I ever loved in my life.

I admired and loved you almost since the day we first met at Cornell …

What a treat it has been to watch you progress to the very top of the legal world.

I will be in here until Friday and, between then and now, I shall think hard on my remaining health and life, and whether on balance the time has come for me to tough it out or to take leave of life because the loss of quality now simply overwhelms.'

I hold my breath.
My legs start to shake.

The paper takes on a surreal quality.
The writing is his but it is not.

MARTY: 'I hope you will support where I come out, but I understand you may not.'

I hear a howl.
I realize it is me.

MARTY: 'I will not love you a jot less.'

Life stands still.

When he comes home on Friday,
I am there.

On Sunday he takes his last breath.

After fifty-nine years together
I am without my Marty.

She folds into herself with deeply felt loss.

TRANSITION BETWEEN PARTS TWO AND THREE

Heather Mitchell in Sydney Theatre Company's RBG: Of Many, One*, 2023 (Photo: Prudence Upton)*

PART THREE

2012

Work-out music followed by opera.

RUTH *is conducting her version of a personal training session.*

Small weights and steps—plus big gym balls.

At my advanced age
I am finally working out.
And I love it.

The Canadian army workout.

'Who's the most important person in my life?' they asked me at Stanford.

RUTH: 'Bryant Johnson.
My personal trainer.'

Because it is he who is keeping me alive for everything else.

Twenty sit-ups a day,
ten then breathe then another ten, breathe.

And up.

A year after my lunch with Obama there's a huge landmark decision.
I was angry.
The majority got their judgment very very wrong.

Burwell versus Hobby Lobby Stores.
The Green family owns and operates five hundred arts and crafts stores.
Hobby Lobby Stores.
But explicit Christian faith says contraception is immoral.
And so they won't allow employees' healthcare to cover contraception.

And one, two, three—

She continues her weights.

Religious freedom versus women's rights.
My dissent is strong.

RUTH: 'A profit company is not a religious organistion. The ability of women to participate equally in the economic and social life of the nation, has been facilitated by their ability to control their reproductive lives.'

I write all my dissent judgments in full, unlike other judges who write short dissents, carefully covering all my bases.
I need them to be heard.

They must be foolproof.
Direct.
Stronger than ever.
Fuelled by my fury.

She works out.

It's very important to hydrate. I find working out at lunchtime puts a real zing in the afternoon.

This new zeal—things are exciting.

Lunch with Obama at the White House has changed me.

My judicial robes might be smaller than everyone else
but what I say in them carries just as much weight,
even when I am in dissent!

This is a new world
change is possible
and I know that my dissents can lead a path.

I wear my spiky bejeweled collar on a black band
from Banana Republic when I am in dissent;
and the egg-yolk yellow crocheted collar
when I am one of the majority—that collar is a gift from my law clerks.

But,
mostly I wear my dissent collar
and my dissenting judgments are
blueprints.
I must be prepared,
for what is coming.

A new president.
A woman.
Soon, I hope.

She will read these dissents.

Take them to Congress
and
will change the laws.

And change this nation.

2015

Oh Marty, I wish you were still here,
I know you would tease me mercilessly.

I'm going to be on the cover of *Time* magazine.
Yes, really.

In the photo I will be wearing one of my collars.
And lace gloves.

Sandra said to me once: 'You're vulnerable now and shaking hands with a lot of people so you should at least wear gloves.'

Laughs.

I know, I know,
quite the image.
Marty, I can see your eyebrows doing that thing they do!

And, Marty
I'm a meme,
Yep, a meme.

They call me the 'Notorious RBG'.

Like the rapper singer,
Clara explained it.

I'm on t-shirts and cups and hats and bags.

People younger than Clara are taking selfies with me.

I feel included.

This new generation wants
to make life better
not just for oneself, but for one's community.

2016

I'm at a dinner party.
I don't know all the guests but it's a pleasant group.
All Democrat supporters.
Still, as a member of the judiciary I must be careful what I say in company.

The talk is all about this joke of a presidential race.
Hillary is doing a marvelous job, ahead in the polls
against this awful Donald Trump man, this New York money-maker.

We see TV footage of him and …

She shakes her head shocked / aghast.

TRUMP: 'I moved on her, actually. I did try and fuck her. She was married—and I moved on her very heavily. I moved on her like a bitch. But I couldn't get there.
She's now got the big phony tits and everything.'

I can't believe what I am hearing!

TRUMP: 'You know, I'm automatically attracted to beautiful—I just start kissing them. It's like a magnet. Just kiss. I don't even wait. And when you're a star, they let you do it.
Grab 'em by the pussy. You can do anything.'

Oh my god, did he say that?!

That's what the actual GOP candidate for the President of the United States of America said!

But something amazing happens,

his words inspire women to roar once again.

There's a massive march.
Women of all ages
descend on every city.

They all wear—pussy hats.
Clara's friend at work, she knitted me one, a pussy hat.
It's pink and it's well a symbol of a …
of women.

Another wave of women speaking out!
Finding their voices,
talking about discrimination;
violence against women.

We are demanding a revolution!
It's electrifying.

It is my great good fortune to be alive during this social revolution.

2016

The presidential debate is on the TV.

Hillary can easily outwit Trump.
How has he even made it this far?!

But Trump goes for the jugular

as expected.
He doesn't play by the rules.
Good lord this man doesn't even know what the rules are.

Did he just say he would put her in jail?
Does he have any understanding of the law at all?
He clearly has never heard of due process.
The Rule of Law says everyone has a fair trial!
I feel my blood boil.

Everyone speaks out.

I speak out.

I tell *The Times*.

RUTH: 'I don't even want to contemplate four years of a Trump presidency and the effect it could have on the court.'

To the *Associated Press* I say:

RUTH: 'The next president will be Hillary.'

And to CNN:

RUTH: 'He needs to turn over his tax returns, he is not above the law.'

And then I say:

RUTH: 'He has no consistency about him. He says whatever comes into his head at the moment. Trump is a faker with an ego.'

The next morning

I wake up,

and Trump has tweeted …

2016

TRUMP: 'Resign.
She's lost her mind!
Justice Ginsburg's mind is shot—resign!'

The newspapers jump in:
'Justice Ginsburg has crossed the line.'

CNN blaring: 'Her comments were out of place.'

Others are calling: 'Time out for Justice Ginsburg.'

The House Speaker says: 'For someone who is going to be calling balls and strikes in the future based upon whatever Congress does, that strikes me as inherently biased and out of the realm.'

I don't care.

I have no regrets—and I'm bored with the sports analogies.

I said it loud and clear. And I meant it.

I refuse to apologize,
because it's true.

Tweets keep coming:
'She believes her own hype.'

'She thinks she IS notorious.'

'How dare she? A judge interfering with Congress.'

'Judges should not be celebrities; she's forgotten her place.'

What if he gets in.
I, I …

He won't.
He can't.
He's a clown, a fool.

I tell myself:

'Hillary is in the lead.'

And yet.

I told Obama not to meddle in the court,
I said: 'Just as a judge like me should never meddle in the workings of Congress.'

And …
Now,

I have done that very thing.

I have interfered
where no judge should.

That fury of mine.

RUTH: [*to Marty*] 'Oh Marty. I wish you were here.
They are saying I like my new image too much,
my notoriety.'

The Chief Justice calls me in.

I must resign or apologize.
I can't resign when Hillary is just about to take office.

How did I let myself do this?

A judge stepped into the political realm.
And, and
I was that judge.

Oh my god, I am so ashamed.

I feel so humiliated.

Beat.

She gathers herself despite her fury.

I must
apologize to Mr Trump.

RUTH: 'On reflection, my recent remarks in response to press inquiries were ill-advised and I regret making them. Judges should avoid commenting on a candidate for public office. In the future I will be more circumspect.'

The only time in my career
when I favored emotion
over process.

And so publicly.

I am so ashamed of myself and.

This fallibility …
it hurts.

2016 Tuesday November 8

Election Night

My granddaughter Clara is beside me when everything is lost.

Clara is weeping.

CLARA: 'Don't concede, Hillary.'
She calls out to the television.

Hillary concedes.

And to our silent and absolute horror,
Donald Trump steps up as the forty-fifth president of the United States of America.

Trump is gloating.
Obama speaks:

OBAMA: 'It is no secret the president-elect and I have some pretty significant differences,
nevertheless, we are all rooting for Mr Trump to succeed in his new role.'

And yet,
the years that follow are unimaginable.

I'm counting down Trump's four years in office
I will survive them all.

I fall over in my office,
fracture three ribs.
Doctors investigate
and …
tumors.
But I am strong.

I am fighting on all fronts
but my cancer is metastasizing.

I will not die while Trump is in office. I cannot.

I have worked too hard and too long
to let him choose my replacement.

I will stay alive, and I will stay in court.

Was I guilty of too much hope?

Fifty-five days left of his term.
Before the election.

MARTY: 'Hold on, Kiki, hold on.'

What if I cannot hold on?

RUTH: 'Oh Marty.'

2020 Friday September 18

Washington DC

Forty-six days until the election. Trump versus Biden.

Clara snuggles close.

CLARA: 'This election will be different, Bubbie.'

Trump must lose.

I wonder how many more breaths there are in forty-six days.

RUTH: 'Clara? How many breaths?'

One of James's daughters gets out her calculator
until James shoos her out.

Laughs.

Jane bends over me.
My strong, beautiful daughter,
so like her father.
Forty-six days.
Counting down until the election.

I feel pain mixed with morphine—a strange timelessness.

I suddenly know this will be my final night.
I realize this is my deathbed,
like Marty before me
and Celia before that.
Like my sister
Marilyn Elsa Bader
in a tiny grave in Queens.

This time I will not beat it.
We all have our last fight.
Clara touches my forehead.

CLARA: 'You don't have to fight, Bubbie.'

She says.

Beat.

She is brave—I hold my legacy in this young woman. Descendant of Marty and me.

RUTH: 'Darling, here is only one thing I am not resolved about.'

She assumes it is that I never resigned for Obama.

No. No.
My best work was done in my furious dissents after that lunch.

RUTH: 'Clara, I regret speaking out in warning of Trump.
But it is comforting to know that my words had no effect on changing the democratic outcome.
He still was voted in.

The constitution only allows me to maintain my judicial position as long as I am fit and able.
And now, I am no longer fit and able.
So therefore, I am no longer a sitting judge giving opinion.
And as such I am allowed to speak out now!

Darling, I want to dictate something to you.

[*Dictating*] "My final wish is that I am not replaced in my role on the Supreme Court of the United States of America until such time as the election has been won. That the vacancy that now exists at my incapacity, is held until the upcoming election result is determined.”

And, Clara, I make this final wish on behalf of
we,
the people.

And in particular,
we, the women.’

I know that there will be women leaders in that future,
women presidents and judges reading my road map,
discussing my dissents.

I can hear their voices loud, clear and ringing out.

It becomes music
ice shards in my mouth.
The morphine goes in again
swimming in my blood.
Clara cradles my head.
I look at Clara and she becomes Jane who becomes Celia.

Marty walks towards me
smiling.

He puts out his arm.

RUTH: ‘Marty!’

I cling to him,
and I’m dancing with Marty.
He’s laughing, sweeping me off the floor.

Before finally,
finally.

The music becomes distilled to a lone operatic voice,
singing a capella.
There is warmth in my veins,
my blood is slowly, very gently pumping,
I can hear it
from the inside.

My heart soars
and I breathe in this world
one more time;
infused with a merging,
a oneness with everything.

A song of joy
of fulfillment
of love.

Of life.

RUTH *stands and looks right out to the audience.*

A tiny eighty-year-old woman, one of so many.

A gentle smile emerges on her lips.

Then.

Lights down.

THE END